CW00350231

A taste of

Italian proverbs collected and curated
by John Stewart

Table of Contents

What makes a proverb a proverb?

There isn't just one definition for "proverb."

Defining proverbs and interpreting their meanings are daunting tasks, and academics have dedicated their careers to describing their properties. Lord John Russell remarked that proverbs could be considered as the "wit of one and the wisdom of many;" Wolfgang Mieder gave a more definitive description, characterizing the proverb as a "short, well-known sentence that conveys wisdom, truth, morals and traditional views in a metaphorical and memorizable form."

Good enough for me. I've lived and worked on every continent except Antarctica and studied more than 30 languages over the past three decades; collecting proverbs was a means of expanding my vocabulary and understanding of a culture. While I still enjoy the vocabularic souvenirs embedded in proverbs, it became more important to glean wisdom from their meaning to apply to real life. And, in promoting proverbs through my works, I've found purpose in their collection, curation and preservation for future generations.

What our sayings say about us

Proverbs encapsulate what a society perceives as wisdom, and can offer practical advice to navigate life's complexities, even at the risk of oversimplifying or misapplying their meanings. Independent of their utility, however, proverbs are important clues to how people in the past made sense of the world around them, and point to the values and beliefs of a culture.

Maybe most importantly, proverbs touch on themes like love, grief, fear, ambition and hope, illustrating the commonalities that exist across different cultures and time periods and pointing to a universal human experience that underpins every society - we may feel alone, but we are never as alone as we think we are.

This book is a companion for the slightly more sophisticated traveler, a cornucopia of vocabulary for the language learner and a guide for knowledge seekers. It can hitch a ride in a backpack or collect dust on a coffee table; its pages are destined to be dogeared and occasionally visited by the curious, the restless and those seeking their next step on their personal path of enlightenment. I know I am.

Italian's place in the world

More than 60 million people speak Italian as their first language as the official language of Italy, but it is also widely spoken as a second language by millions of people in neighboring countries such as Switzerland, Slovenia, and Croatia, and in parts of the rest of the world, from the Americas to Oceania and places in between.

Its rich history needs little introduction; its influence is all around us in literature, music, and cuisine, from pizza and pasta to some of the greatest works of world literature, including Dante's *Divine Comedy* and Boccaccio's *The Decameron*. Its contributions helped shape the development of similar languages like Spanish, French, Portuguese, and Romanian, among many others, and those cultural contributions, along with its entrancing geography and Mediterranean climate, are part of why Italy receives approximately 60 million tourists every year- roughly the size of its own population.

"Saper non è conoscenza, saper d'averla è."

"Knowledge is not wisdom; to know that one has it is wisdom."

- *Petrarch (Francesco Petrarca)*

Italian proverbs

A buon intenditor poche parole.

Few words are enough for a good listener.

Smart people can understand things with only a few hints.

A caval donato non si guarda in bocca.

Don't look a gift horse in the mouth.

Don't be ungrateful for something given to you for free.

A chi dorme il mondo appartiene.

The world belongs to those who sleep.

Those who are inactive and unproductive

will not achieve their goals.

A chi dorme non arriva fortuna.

Fortune doesn't come to those who sleep.

You need to work hard and be alert to seize opportunities.

A chi dorme non arriva mai fortuna.

Fortune never comes to those who sleep.

Success requires hard work and effort.

A chi fa male, mai mancano scuse.

Those who do harm, never lack excuses.

People who do wrong often try to justify their actions.

A chi vuole, non mancano modi.

For those who want it, there are no shortages of ways.

When someone is determined to achieve something, they will find a way to make it happen.

A ogni morte di papa.

Every pope's death.

This expression is used to describe something that happens very rarely.

A ogni uccello il suo nido è bello.

Every bird thinks its own nest is beautiful.

Everyone thinks their own home or country is the best.

Acqua passata non macina più.

The past water does not grind anymore.

What's done is done and cannot be undone.

Avere le mani bucate.

To have holes in one's hands.

To be bad with money and spend it quickly.

Bisogna lavorare per vivere, non vivere per lavorare.

One should work to live, not live to work.

Work should not consume someone's entire life.

Bisogna mettere la testa a posto.

You have to put your head in place.

People need to focus and concentrate on

their goals.

Bisogna prendere il toro per le corna.

You have to take the bull by the horns.

You have to take charge of a situation and face it head-on.

Bisogna saper perdere per poter vincere.

You have to know how to lose to be able to win.

Learning from losses and failures can lead to greater success in the future.

Buon sangue non mente.

Good blood doesn't lie.

People's family or heritage can often influence their character or behavior.

Chi ben comincia è a metà dell'opera.

He who begins well is halfway through his task.

Starting something in the right way is crucial to its success.

Chi ben lavora, ben mangia.

He who works well eats well.

Hard work pays off and leads to success.

Chi cerca trova.

He who seeks shall find.

If you actively look for something, you're more likely to find it.

Chi di spada ferisce, di spada perisce.

He who wounds with a sword will die by the sword.

If you hurt someone, you may eventually face consequences.

Chi dorme con i cani si alza con le pulci.

He who sleeps with dogs wakes up with fleas.

If you associate with bad people, you'll likely face negative consequences.

Chi dorme non piglia pesci.

He who sleeps does not catch fish.

If you're not actively working towards something, you're not going to achieve it.

Chi è causa del suo mal, pianga sé stesso.

He who is the cause of his own misfortune, should weep over himself.

People are responsible for their own actions and the consequences that come with them.

Chi fa da sé, fa per tre.

He who does things for himself does the work of three.

Doing things on your own can be more efficient and effective.

Chi ha capo ha cascarelli.

He who has a head has headaches.

Being in a position of responsibility can come with its own problems.

Chi ha ferro ha pane.

He who has iron has bread.

Having resources and tools can lead to greater success and abundance.

Chi ha fretta mangia crudo.

He who is in a hurry eats raw.

Haste can lead to mistakes or negative outcomes.

Chi ha il pane non ha i denti, e chi ha i denti non ha il pane.

He who has bread doesn't have teeth, and he who has teeth doesn't have bread.

Sometimes we have things we can't use, and other times we have the ability to do something but lack the necessary resources.

Chi ha orecchie per intendere, intenda.

He who has ears to hear, let him hear.

People should be open to hearing and understanding the truth.

Chi ha pane non ha denti.

He who has bread has no teeth.

Sometimes we don't appreciate what we have until we no longer have a use for it.

Chi ha pazienza ha tutto.

He who has patience has everything.

Being patient can lead to greater success and fulfillment in life.

Chi ha tempo non aspetti tempo.

He who has time shouldn't wait for time.

If you have the opportunity to do something, don't wait too long to do it.

Chi ha un amico ha un tesoro.

He who has a friend has a treasure.

Having good friends can be invaluable.

Chi ha un dente contro qualcuno cerca di mangiarselo.

He who has a grudge against someone tries to eat it.

People who hold grudges seek revenge or vindication.

Chi ha un perché ha un percome.

He who has a why has a how.

Having a clear purpose or motivation can

lead to success and a plan for achieving it.

Chi ha una buona moglie, ha un buon tesoro.

He who has a good wife has a good treasure.

Having a supportive and loving spouse can be invaluable.

Chi la dura la vince.

He who perseveres wins.

Persistence and determination can lead to success.

Chi la fa l'aspetti.

Whoever does it, waits for it.

Negative actions have negative consequences.

Chi lascia la via vecchia per la nuova, sa quel che lascia ma non quel che trova.

He who leaves the old path for the new one knows what he leaves but not what he finds.

Changing something familiar for something unknown can be risky.

Chi nasce tondo non muore quadrato.

He who is born round does not die square.

People's innate characteristics and tendencies don't change over time.

Chi non fa non falla.

He who doesn't act doesn't make mistakes.

People who avoid taking action can avoid making mistakes, but they also miss out on opportunities.

Chi non lavora non fa l'amore.

He who doesn't work doesn't make love.

Working hard can lead to greater rewards in all areas of life.

Chi non lavora non mangia.

He who doesn't work doesn't eat.

You need to work to earn a living and provide for yourself and your family.

Chi non risica non rosica.

He who doesn't take risks doesn't get to nibble.

Taking risks is necessary to achieve success or gain a reward.

Chi più sa meno crede.

He who knows more believes less.

People who are knowledgeable and experienced are less likely to be fooled or misled.

Chi più spende meno pensa.

He who spends more thinks less.

People who are focused on spending money may not be as thoughtful about their purchases.

Chi semina vento raccoglie tempesta.

He who sows wind reaps a storm.

If you do something negative, it will likely come back to you in a much more intense and damaging way.

Chi si accontenta gode.

He who is content enjoys.

Being satisfied with what we have leads to happiness.

Chi si ferma è perduto.

He who stops is lost.

It's important to keep moving forward in order to achieve success.

Chi si somiglia si piglia.

Birds of a feather flock together.

People with similar personalities or interests often associate with each other.

Chi tace acconsente.

Silence gives consent.

Silence can indicate agreement or approval.

Chi tardi arriva, male alloggia.

He who arrives late, lodges poorly.

If you don't plan ahead, you may end up with undesirable options.

Chi troppo vuole nulla stringe.

He who wants too much ends up with nothing.

Being too greedy can lead to losing everything.

Chi trova un amico trova un tesoro.

He who finds a friend finds a treasure.

Having good friends is valuable and enriching.

Chi va con lo zoppo, impara a zoppicare.

He who walks with the lame learns to limp.

Associating with people who have bad habits can lead to adopting those habits.

Chi va piano va sano e va lontano.

He who goes slowly goes safely and goes far.

Taking your time and being cautious will help you succeed in the long run.

Chi vuol pecora, si tosca.

He who wants a sheep should shear it.

If you want something, you need to put in the effort to get it.

Chi vuole la rosa deve sopportare le spine.

He who wants the rose must endure the thorns.

To achieve something worthwhile, you may have to put up with hardships and challenges.

Conosci te stesso.

Know thyself.

Self-awareness is important for personal growth and development.

Cosa fatta capo ha.

A thing done has a head.

Actions have consequences.

Dalle stelle alle stalle.

From the stars to the stables.

This expression describes someone who was once successful but has since fallen from grace.

Dobbiamo imparare ad aspettare il momento giusto per agire.

We must learn to wait for the right moment to act.

Timing is important for success.

Dove c'è fumo, c'è fuoco.

Where there's smoke, there's fire.

If there are rumors or gossip about something, there's likely some truth to it.

Fatti non foste a viver come bruti, ma per seguir virtute e conoscenza.

You were not made to live like beasts, but to follow virtue and knowledge.

This quote from Dante's "Divine Comedy" encourages people to strive for knowledge and morality.

Fidarsi è bene, non fidarsi è meglio.

Trusting is good, not trusting is better.

It's important to be cautious and not blindly trust others.

Gli amici degli amici miei sono miei amici.

My friends' friends are my friends.

Building relationships with people through mutual connections is common.

I cari estinti hanno molte pretese.

The dear departed have many demands.

People who have passed away are often spoken of positively, regardless of their faults.

I problemi non sono problemi ma sono sfide.

Problems are not problems, but challenges.

Seeing problems as opportunities for growth and improvement can lead to a positive mindset.

I sogni son desideri.

Dreams are desires.

Dreams can be a reflection of our deepest desires.

I soldi non danno la felicità.

Money doesn't bring happiness.

True happiness comes from within and can't be bought.

I veri amici si vedono nel momento del bisogno.

True friends are seen in times of need.

Real friends are there to help and support during difficult times.

Il buongiorno si vede dal mattino.

The good day is seen from the morning.

The beginning of something often sets the tone for the rest of it.

Il cuore ha le sue ragioni che la ragione

non conosce.

The heart has its reasons that reason doesn't know.

Sometimes our emotions and feelings dictate our decisions more than rational thinking.

Il denaro non fa la felicità.

Money doesn't bring happiness.

Happiness cannot be bought with money.

Il destino batte la porta, ma il caso ci fa incontrare.

Destiny knocks on the door, but chance makes us meet.

While we may have a certain fate, chance encounters and events can alter our paths.

Il diavolo fa le pentole ma non i coperchi.

The devil makes the pots, but not the lids.

Everyone has their weaknesses or blind spots, even if they seem perfect in other areas.

Il diavolo sta nei dettagli.

The devil is in the details.

Small details can be very important and make a big difference.

Il fine giustifica i mezzi.

The end justifies the means.

Sometimes it's acceptable to do something unethical in order to achieve a greater good.

Il gioco è bello finché dura.

The game is fun as long as it lasts.

Enjoyment can be fleeting and temporary.

Il giusto mezzo è il miglior partito.

The happy medium is the best match.

Finding balance and moderation leads to greater success and happiness.

Il giusto mezzo è la virtù.

The right balance is the virtue.

Finding a balance in life is important for personal growth and success.

Il lavoro nobilita l'uomo.

Work dignifies man.

Working hard and earning a living can lead to a sense of self-worth and accomplishment.

Il lupo perde il pelo ma non il vizio.

The wolf may lose its fur, but not its nature.

Someone's bad habits or character traits will likely stay with them even if they try to change.

Il male non viene mai da solo.

Evil never comes alone.

One negative situation can often lead to more problems.

Il mare non bagna il monte.

The sea doesn't wet the mountain.

Sometimes, we have to accept that certain

things are beyond our control.

Il mattino ha l'oro in bocca.

The morning has gold in its mouth.

Mornings are often the most productive or successful time of the day.

Il meglio è nemico del bene.

The best is the enemy of the good.

Sometimes trying to achieve perfection can prevent you from making progress or achieving success.

Il mondo è bello perché è vario.

The world is beautiful because it is diverse.

Differences and diversity can add beauty and interest to the world.

Il mondo è un fazzoletto.

The world is a handkerchief.

This expression suggests that people are
more connected than they realize.

Il pane degli altri è sempre più buono.

Other people's bread is always tastier.

People often envy what others have and
take for granted what they have
themselves.

Il pane di ieri è quello che sa di meglio.

Yesterday's bread is the best.

Things often taste better when they're not
fresh or new.

Il pane quotidiano.

Daily bread.

This expression describes the basic necessities of life, such as food and shelter.

Il peccato abita accanto.

Sin lives next door.

People who do bad things are often close to us.

Il peccato morde il cielo.

Sin bites the sky.

Doing something bad will eventually catch up to you.

Il pesce puzza dalla testa.

The fish stinks from the head.

Poor leadership or management can cause problems throughout an organization.

Il piacere della vita è la libertà.

The pleasure of life is freedom.

Having the ability to make choices and live freely is essential to happiness.

Il piacere più dolce è quello che si aspetta.

The sweetest pleasure is the one that is anticipated.

Anticipation can make something even more enjoyable.

Il primo amore non si scorda mai.

You never forget your first love.

The first person you fall in love with can

hold a special place in your heart.

Il primo passo è il più difficile.

The first step is the most difficult.

Starting something new can be the most challenging part.

Il rispetto dei diritti degli altri è la pace.

Respect for the rights of others is peace.

Treating others with respect and fairness can lead to peaceful relationships.

Il rispetto è reciproco.

Respect is mutual.

Mutual respect is important for

Il silenzio è d'oro.

Silence is golden.

Sometimes it's better to remain silent than to say something that could cause harm.

Il sole dietro le nuvole splende sempre.

The sun always shines behind the clouds.

Even in difficult situations, there is hope for a better outcome.

Il successo ha molti padri, ma il fallimento è orfano.

Success has many fathers, but failure is an orphan.

People are often quick to take credit for success, but distance themselves from failure.

Il tempo è denaro.

Time is money.

Time is a valuable resource that should be used wisely.

Il tempo è galantuomo.

Time is a gentleman.

Over time,

In bocca al lupo!

In the mouth of the wolf!

This is a common expression used to wish someone good luck.

In un batter d'occhio.

In the blink of an eye.

Something happens very quickly or

suddenly.

L'abito non fa il monaco.

The habit doesn't make the monk.

Appearances can be deceiving, and you
can't judge someone based solely on their
appearance.

L'abitudine fa il monaco.

Habit makes the monk.

Repeated actions and habits shape a
person's character.

L'abitudine non fa la monaca.

Habit doesn't make the nun.

Repeated actions and habits don't define a
person's character.

L'albero cade sempre dal lato dove pende di più.

The tree always falls on the side where it leans the most.

People or things that are the most unbalanced are the most likely to fall.

L'amore non ha età.

Love has no age.

Love can be found at any age or stage of life.

L'apparenza inganna.

Appearance deceives.

People should not be judged solely on their appearance.

L'appetito vien mangiando.

Appetite comes with eating.

The more you do something, the more you want to do it.

L'arte è lunga, la vita è breve.

Art is long, life is short.

There is a lot to learn and master, but time is limited.

L'esperienza è la madre della saggezza.

Experience is the mother of wisdom.

Experience leads to knowledge and wisdom.

L'occasione fa l'uomo ladro.

Opportunity makes the man a thief.

When presented with a tempting opportunity, people may be inclined to do something dishonest.

L'ospite è come il pesce: dopo tre giorni puzza.

A guest is like a fish: after three days it stinks.

Guests can become unwelcome or overstay their welcome if they stay too long.

L'unica cosa che ci separa dai sogni è la volontà di realizzarli.

The only thing that separates us from our dreams is the will to achieve them.

Success requires motivation and determination.

L'unione fa la forza.

Unity makes strength.

Working together can lead to greater
success and strength.

La bellezza è relativa.

Beauty is relative.

Beauty is subjective and varies from person
to person.

La bellezza sta negli occhi di chi guarda.

Beauty is in the eye of the beholder.

Beauty is subjective and varies from person
to person.

La buona volontà è la metà dell'opera.

Goodwill is half the battle.

Having a positive attitude and a willingness to work hard can lead to success.

La casa del vicino è sempre più verde.

The neighbor's grass is always greener.

People may be envious of what others have, even if they have their own blessings.

La conoscenza è potere.

Knowledge is power.

Having knowledge and information can lead to greater success and influence.

La donna è mobile.

Woman is fickle.

This expression suggests that women can be unpredictable.

La fama costa cara.

Fame costs dearly.

Achieving fame or success can come at a high price.

La fame è il miglior condimento.

Hunger is the best seasoning.

When we are hungry, even simple foods can taste delicious.

La fatica è amara, ma i suoi frutti sono dolci.

Hard work is bitter, but its fruits are sweet.

Working hard can lead to greater rewards in all areas of life.

La felicità è fatta di piccole cose.

Happiness is made up of small things.

Appreciating the little things in life can lead to greater overall happiness.

La felicità non è un premio, ma un viaggio.

Happiness is not a reward, but a journey.

Happiness is a continuous process and not a one-time achievement.

La felicità non si compra con il denaro.

Happiness cannot be bought with money.

True happiness comes from within and cannot be purchased.

La fortuna aiuta gli audaci.

Fortune favors the bold.

Those who take risks and are brave may be rewarded in life.

La fortuna bacia gli audaci.

Fortune kisses the bold.

Taking risks and being daring can lead to success.

La fortuna è cieca, ma la sfortuna vede lontano.

Luck is blind, but misfortune sees far.

When things are going well, people may not see potential problems, but when things go wrong, they can see them clearly.

La furbizia è la prima forma di intelligenza.

Cleverness is the first form of intelligence.

Being clever and resourceful can be a valuable skill.

La gatta ci cova.

The cat is hatching something.

This expression suggests that someone is plotting something.

La gatta frettolosa fa i gattini ciechi.

The hasty cat has blind kittens.

Rushing or being too hasty can lead to mistakes or problems.

La lontananza fa aumentare l'amore.

Distance makes love grow.

Being separated from someone can

intensify feelings of love and affection.

La luce più splendente è quella del sole.

The brightest light is that of the sun.

The most important or powerful entity is often the most obvious or apparent.

La necessità aguzza l'ingegno.

Necessity sharpens ingenuity.

People can become more creative and resourceful when faced with difficult circumstances.

La notte porta consiglio.

The night brings counsel.

Taking time to reflect on a situation can lead to better decision-making.

La paura fa novanta.

Fear makes ninety.

Fear can exaggerate a situation or make it seem worse than it is.

La pazienza è la virtù dei forti.

Patience is the virtue of the strong.

Being patient requires strength and perseverance.

La pratica fa il maestro.

Practice makes perfect.

Repeated practice leads to improvement and mastery.

La pratica rende perfetti.

Practice makes perfect.

Consistent effort can lead to mastery.

La prudenza è la virtù dei saggi.

Prudence is the virtue of the wise.

Being cautious and careful leads to better decision-making.

La ripetizione è la madre della memoria.

Repetition is the mother of memory.

Repeating something leads to better memory and retention.

La solitudine è cara ma l'amicizia è ancora più cara.

Solitude is expensive, but friendship is even more expensive.

Good friendships are valuable and worth investing in.

La speranza è l'ultima a morire.

Hope is the last to die.

Even in difficult situations, people can hold onto hope for a better outcome.

La verità è come l'olio, viene sempre in superficie.

Truth is like oil, it always rises to the surface.

The truth will always be revealed eventually.

La verità sta in mezzo.

The truth lies in the middle.

The truth can often be found in a balanced

or moderate view.

La verità vi renderà liberi.

The truth will set you free.

Being honest and truthful can lead to a sense of freedom and release.

La virtù sta nel mezzo.

Virtue lies in the middle.

Finding a balance between extremes is often the best way to live your life.

La vita è come un bicchiere di vino: bisogna saperla gustare.

Life is like a glass of wine: you have to know how to savor it.

Life should be appreciated and enjoyed.

La vita è come un'altalena: bisogna saperla bilanciare.

Life is like a swing: you have to know how to balance it.

Maintaining balance and equilibrium is important for a successful life.

La vita è come un'opera teatrale: non è la lunghezza ma la qualità a contare.

Life is like a play: it's not the length, but the quality that counts.

The quality of one's experiences is more important than the quantity.

La vita è come una scatola di cioccolatini, non sai mai quello che ti capita.

Life is like a box of chocolates, you never know what you're going to get.

Life is unpredictable and full of surprises.

La vita è un dono prezioso.

Life is a precious gift.

Life is valuable and should be appreciated.

La vita è un viaggio, non una destinazione.

Life is a journey, not a destination.

The process of life is more important than the end goal.

La vita è un'opera d'arte che si compone giorno per giorno.

Life is a work of art that is composed day by day.

People have the power to shape their own

lives and make them into something beautiful.

Le belle parole non pascon i gatti.

Pretty words don't feed cats.

Promises or flattery won't actually help someone in need.

Le belle parole non pascono i gatti.

Pretty words don't feed cats.

Actions speak louder than words.

Le cose belle sono difficili.

Beautiful things are difficult.

Achieving something worthwhile often takes hard work and effort.

Le parole sono femmine, i fatti sono maschi.

Words are female, deeds are male.

Actions speak louder than words.

Le promesse si sa, son come le rose di maggio.

Promises, you know, are like May roses.

Promises are often made easily but not kept.

Le vie del Signore sono infinite.

The Lord's ways are infinite.

This expression suggests that there are many ways to achieve a goal.

Lontano dagli occhi, lontano dal cuore.

Out of sight, out of mind.

If you don't see or think about something, you may forget about it.

Meglio soli che male accompagnati.

Better alone than in bad company.

It's better to be alone than in the company of negative or harmful people.

Meglio tardi che mai.

Better late than never.

It's better to do something later than not at all.

Meglio un giorno da leone che cento da pecora.

One day as a lion is better than a hundred as a sheep.

It's better to have one great moment of glory than a lifetime of mediocrity.

Meglio un uomo solo che mal accompagnato.

Better alone than poorly accompanied.

Being alone is better than being in the company of people who are harmful to you.

Meglio un uovo oggi che una gallina domani.

Better an egg today than a chicken tomorrow.

It's better to have something small now than to wait for something bigger that may never come.

Meglio un'ora di matrimonio che una vita di convivenza.

One hour of marriage is better than a lifetime of cohabitation.

Formal commitment is better than living together without any commitment.

Non c'è amore senza gelosia.

There's no love without jealousy.

Romantic love can often bring feelings of jealousy.

Non c'è due senza tre.

There's no two without three.

Things often happen in a sequence of three.

Non c'è fumo senza fuoco.

There's no smoke without fire.

There's usually some truth to rumors or gossip.

Non c'è niente di nuovo sotto il sole.

There's nothing new under the sun.

There are no new ideas, everything has been done before.

Non c'è peggior sordo di chi non vuol sentire.

There's no worse deaf than one who doesn't want to hear.

People who refuse to listen or accept advice can't be helped.

Non c'è rosa senza spine.

There's no rose without thorns.

Everything has its pros and cons, and nothing is perfect.

Non è bello ciò che è bello, ma è bello ciò che piace.

It's not beautiful what is beautiful, but what pleases.

Beauty is subjective and personal.

Non è tutto oro quello che luccica.

Not everything that shines is gold.

Things may appear to be perfect or valuable, but they may not be.

Non fare agli altri ciò che non vorresti fosse fatto a te.

Don't do to others what you wouldn't want done to you.

Treat others the way you would like to be treated.

Non fare agli altri ciò che non vuoi che gli altri facciano a te.

Don't do to others what you don't want done to you.

Treat others how you would like to be treated.

Non fare il passo più lungo della gamba.

Don't take a step longer than your leg.

It's important to be realistic about one's abilities and limitations.

Non giudicare un libro dalla copertina.

Don't judge a book by its cover.

Don't make assumptions about someone or

something based solely on appearances.

Non mettere tutti gli uova nello stesso paniere.

Don't put all your eggs in one basket.

Diversification and spreading risk leads to greater success and stability.

Non si può avere la botte piena e la moglie ubriaca.

You can't have a full barrel and a drunk wife.

You can't have everything you want in life.

Non si può far di un'ape miele e di una mosca aceto.

You can't make honey out of a fly and vinegar out of a bee.

People have inherent qualities and can't be changed.

Non si può insegnare a un vecchio scimmia a fare le fusa.

You can't teach an old monkey to purr.

It's difficult to teach someone who is set in their ways.

Non si vive di solo pane.

One doesn't live on bread alone.

Life isn't just about survival, but also about happiness and fulfillment.

Non tutte le ciambelle riescono col buco.

Not all doughnuts come out with a hole.

Not everything will turn out perfectly, even if

you've done everything right.

Non tutto il male viene per nuocere.

Not all harm comes to hurt.

Sometimes a negative situation can lead to positive outcomes.

Ogni cosa ha il suo prezzo.

Everything has its price.

Everything in life comes with a cost or a consequence.

Ogni cosa ha il suo tempo.

Everything has its time.

Certain events or actions are best done at specific times.

Ogni giorno è una buona giornata per fare del bene.

Every day is a good day to do good.

Doing good deeds and helping others is always valuable.

Ogni medaglia ha il suo rovescio.

Every medal has its reverse side.

Every situation has its positive and negative aspects.

Ogni promessa è debito.

Every promise is a debt.

Promises should be kept and fulfilled.

Ogni scarrafone è bello a mamma sua.

Every cockroach is beautiful in its mother's

eyes.

Parents will always love their children, no matter what they look like or do.

Ogni tanto bisogna perdere per capire quanto è bello vincere.

Sometimes you have to lose to understand how beautiful winning is.

Losing can lead to greater appreciation for success.

Ognuno a casa sua è re.

Each man in his own home is king.

Everyone is in charge of their own domain.

Ognuno è artefice del proprio destino.

Everyone is the architect of their own destiny.

Your choices and actions will determine your future.

Ognuno è artefice della propria fortuna.

Everyone is the architect of their own fortune.

People are responsible for their own success or failure.

Ognuno è artefice della propria sorte.

Everyone is the architect of their own luck.

People are responsible for their own success or failure.

Ognuno è padrone del proprio destino.

Everyone is the master of their own destiny.

People have the power to shape their own

lives and futures.

Ognuno ha la sua croce da portare.

Everyone has their own cross to bear.

Everyone has their own problems and
hardships to deal with.

Ognuno ha la sua opinione.

Everyone has their own opinion.

People are entitled to their own thoughts
and beliefs.

Piove sempre sul bagnato.

It always rains on the wet.

When something bad happens, it's often
compounded by other problems.

Più siamo, più ridiamo.

The more we are, the more we laugh.

Being in the company of others can lead to more joy and laughter.

Prima si prende, meglio è.

The sooner you take it, the better it is.

Acting quickly and decisively can lead to greater success.

Quando il gatto non c'è, i topi ballano.

When the cat's away, the mice dance.

People will often misbehave when there's no one around to hold them accountable.

Quando in Italia non ci fossero le montagne, sarebbe un bellissimo paese.

If there were no mountains in Italy, it would be a beautiful country.

Italy's diverse topography adds to its natural beauty.

Saper perdere è una vittoria.

Knowing how to lose is a victory.

Losing gracefully can be a sign of maturity and strength.

Sbagliando s'impara.

One learns by making mistakes.

Mistakes can be valuable learning opportunities.

Se chiudi una porta, si apre una finestra.

If you close one door, a window opens.

Closing one opportunity can lead to the discovery of new ones.

Se vuoi la pace, preparati alla guerra.

If you want peace, prepare for war.

Being prepared and strong can prevent conflict and deter potential threats.

Se vuoi qualcosa fatto bene, fallo tu stesso.

If you want something done well, do it yourself.

Taking personal responsibility leads to better results.

Si nasce stanchi e si vive per riposare.

We are born tired and we live to rest.

Life can be exhausting and people often

look forward to retirement or rest.

Si può fare di necessità virtù.

Necessity can be the mother of invention.

Difficult situations can inspire creative
solutions.

**Si può portare un cavallo alla fonte, ma
non si può costringerlo a bere.**

*You can bring a horse to water, but you
can't make it drink.*

You can provide someone with an
opportunity, but you can't make them take
it.

Sogni d'oro!

Golden dreams!

This is a common expression used to wish

someone a good night's sleep.

Soldi non portano felicità.

Money doesn't bring happiness.

Wealth doesn't guarantee happiness or fulfillment.

Sotto un cielo di stelle.

Under a sky of stars.

This expression describes a romantic or beautiful setting.

Tra il dire e il fare c'è di mezzo il mare.

Between saying and doing there's the sea.

It's one thing to talk about doing something, but another thing entirely to actually do it.

Tutti i gusti son gusti.

Everyone has their own taste.

People have different preferences and tastes.

Tutto ciò che è fatto con amore è ben fatto.

Everything done with love is well done.

Doing things with passion and love leads to better results.

Tutto è bene ciò che finisce bene.

All is well that ends well.

A successful outcome justifies any difficulties encountered along the way.

Tutto è lecito in guerra e in amore.

Everything is fair in war and love.

Desperate situations can justify extreme actions.

Tutto il mondo è paese.

The whole world is a village.

People and cultures are more similar than they may initially seem.

Un gioco che vale la candela.

A game worth the candle.

Something is worth the effort or expense.

Un sorriso è il miglior make-up che una donna possa indossare.

A smile is the best make-up a woman can wear.

A smile can enhance a person's natural beauty.

Un tiro mancino.

A left-handed shot.

This expression suggests someone has done something sneaky or underhanded.

Un uomo avvisato è mezzo salvato.

A warned man is half saved.

Being aware of potential problems can help avoid them.

Una mano lava l'altra.

One hand washes the other.

People can help each other and benefit from mutual cooperation.

Una mela al giorno toglie il medico di torno.

An apple a day keeps the doctor away.

A healthy diet can prevent illness.

Una rondine non fa primavera.

One swallow doesn't make a spring.

One positive event doesn't mean everything is going to be good.

Made in the USA
Coppell, TX
17 May 2023

16982406R00046